PIANO ACCOMPANIMENT

mel bay presents

christmas solos for trumpet

by william bay

1 2 3 4 5 6 7 8 9 0

Contents

	Trumpet	*Piano*
Angels From The Realms Of Glory	5	8
Angels We Have Heard On High	6	10
As With Gladness Men Of Old	4	6
Away In A Manger	9	18
Coventry Carol	16	34
Ding, Dong, Merrily On High	12	25
The First Nowell	11	22
Good Christian Men, Rejoice	15	32
Hark! The Herald Angels Sing	7	13
I Saw Three Ships	17	36
Joy To The World	13	28
O Come, All Ye Faithful	3	3
Once In David's Royal City	8	16
The Rocking Carol	10	20
Silent Night	14	30

O Come, All Ye Faithful

mp
f
ritard
ritard

As With Gladness Men Of Old

ritard

Angels, From The Realms Of Glory

f

Angels We Have Heard On High

Hark! The Herald Angels Sing

ritard
ritard

Once In David's Royal City

ritard

Away In A Manger

[English Version]

ritard
mf

The Rocking Carol

mel bay presents

christmas solos for trumpet

by william bay

Contents

O Come, All Ye Faithful

As With Gladness Men Of Old

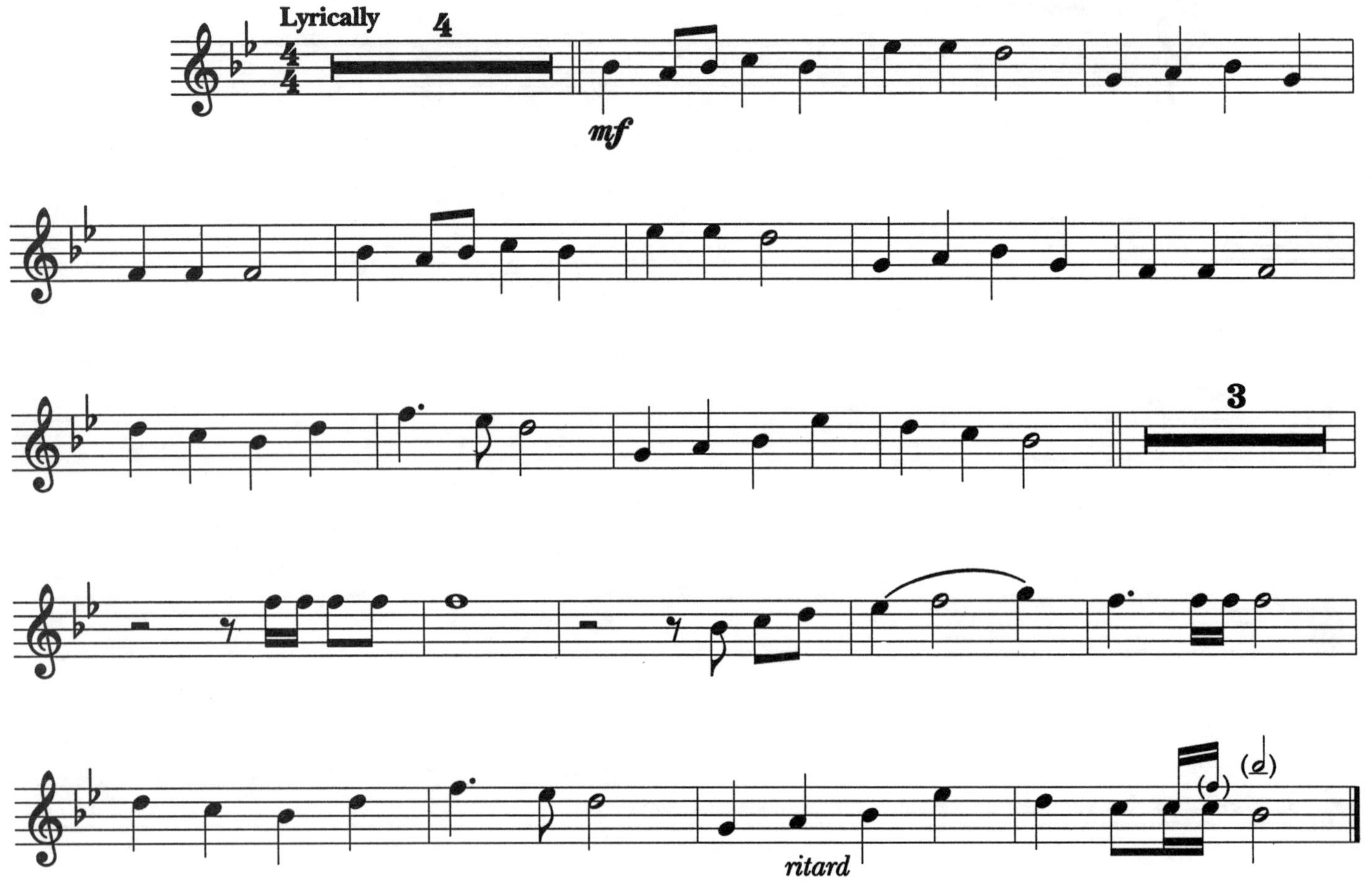

Angels, From The Realms Of Glory

Angels We Have Heard On High

Hark! The Herald Angels Sing

Once In David's Royal City

Away In A Manger
[English Version]

The Rocking Carol

TRUMPET

The First Nowell

Ding, Dong, Merrily On High

Joy To The World

Silent Night

Good Christian Men, Rejoice

Coventry Carol

I Saw Three Ships

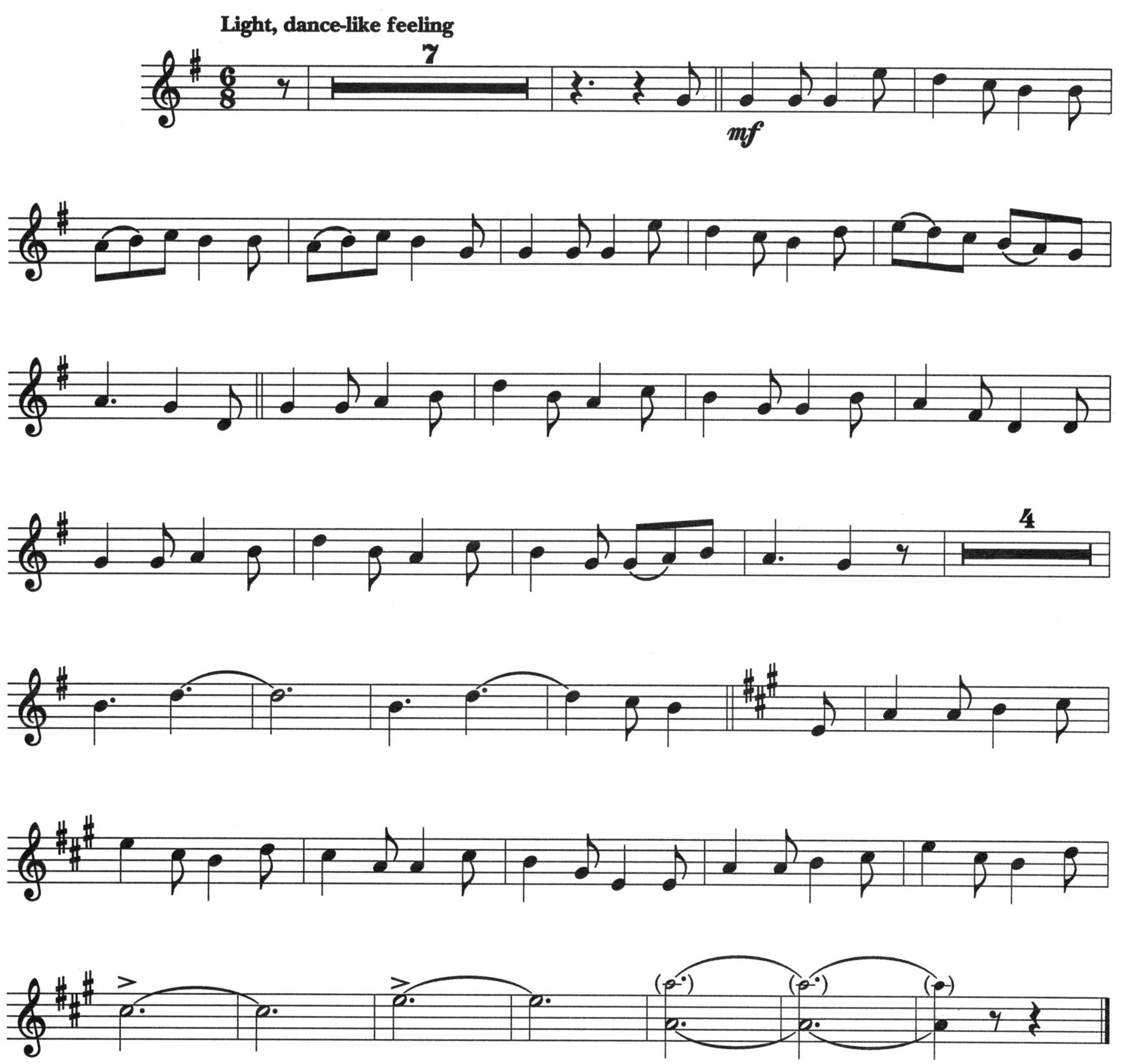

ritard
pp

The First Nowell

f
mf

Ding, Dong, Merrily On High

ritard
ritard
Slower
Slower
Slower
f

Joy To The World

f
ritard
ritard

Silent Night

Good Christian Men, Rejoice

ritard
ritard

Coventry Carol

pp

I Saw Three Ships